BOLD KIDS

Fluorine

EDUCATIONAL FACTS
CHILDREN'S SCIENCE BOOK

Fluorine is a nonmetal element with the atomic number 9 and symbol F. It is the lightest halogen and exists in the form of a pale yellow diatomic gas.

It is highly reactive and the most electronegative element known to science. It reacts with all other elements, except helium and argon.

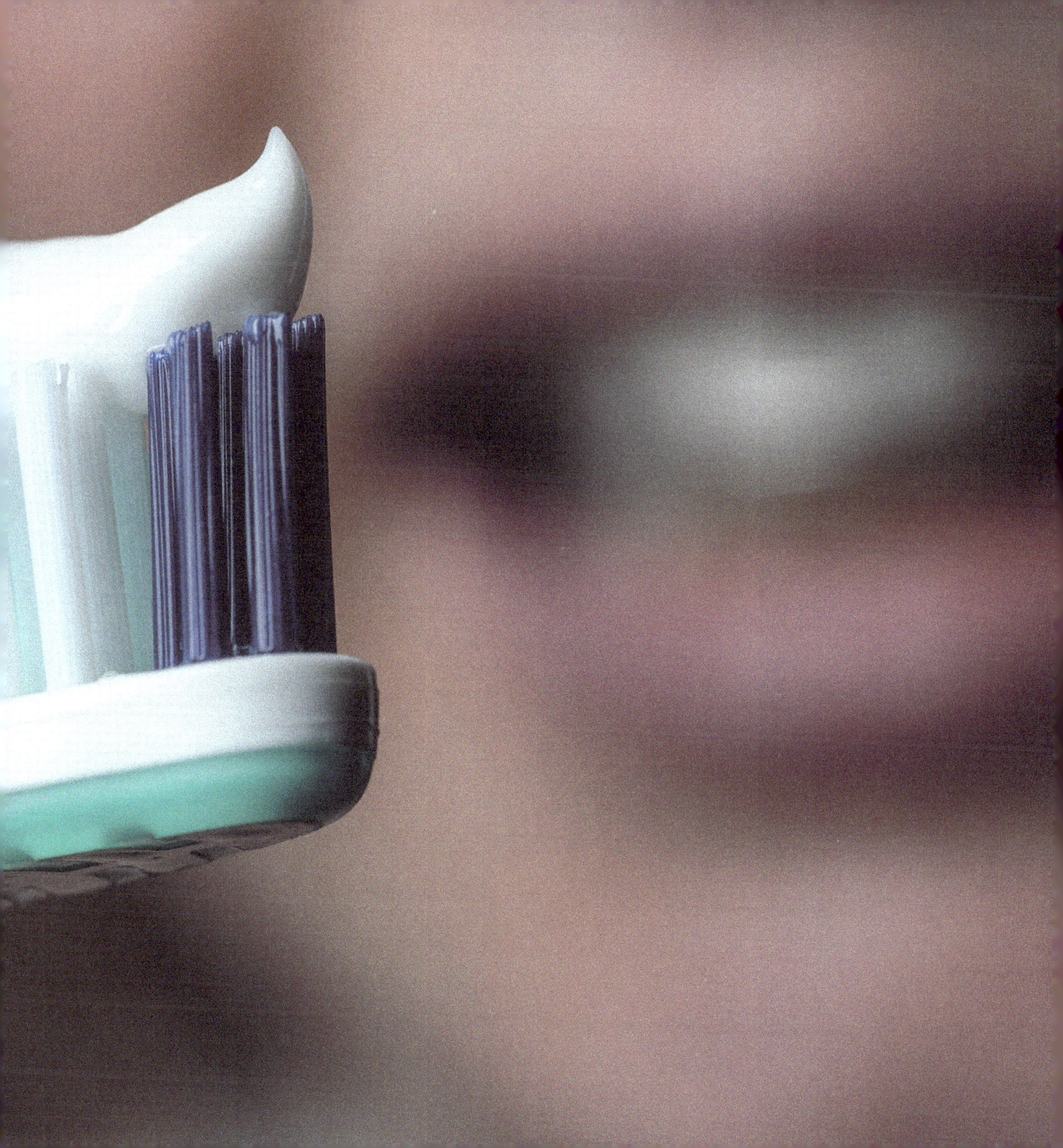

FLUORINE IS A HALOGEN

Fluorine is a chemical element that is part of the halogen family. It is a highly reactive element with an atomic number of nine.

It is the lightest halogen and occurs in the form of a pale yellow diatomic gas. It is the most electronegative element and is very reactive, reacting with all other elements except argon, neon, and helium.

Fluorine is the first element in the group of halogens. It is the lightest of the halogens, with nine protons and nine electrons.

It is the thirteenth most abundant element in the Earth's crust. Fluorine is extremely reactive, and will react with almost every other element in the periodic table. The highest electronegativity is 3.98, meaning that fluorine attracts electrons and is oxidizing.

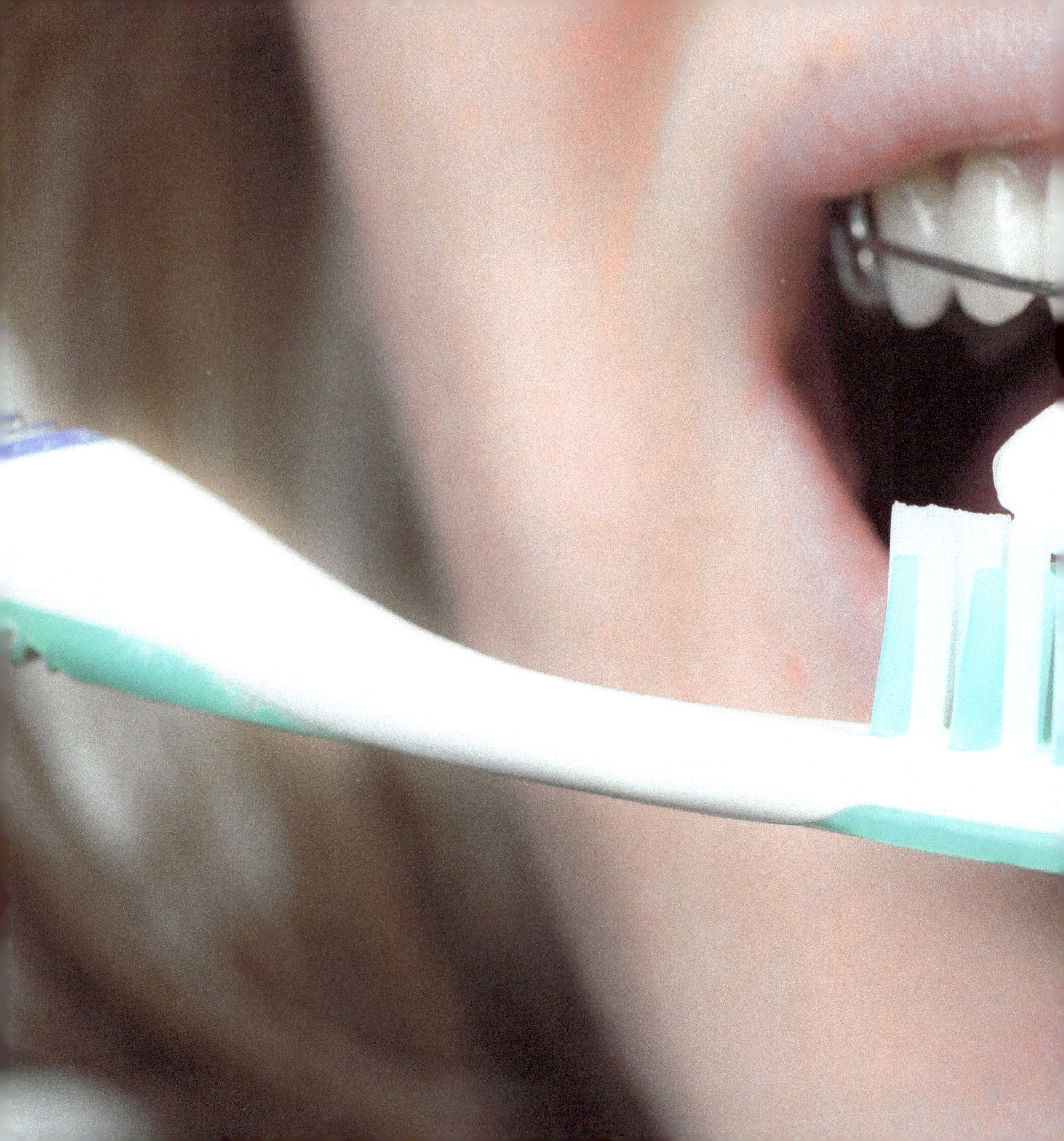

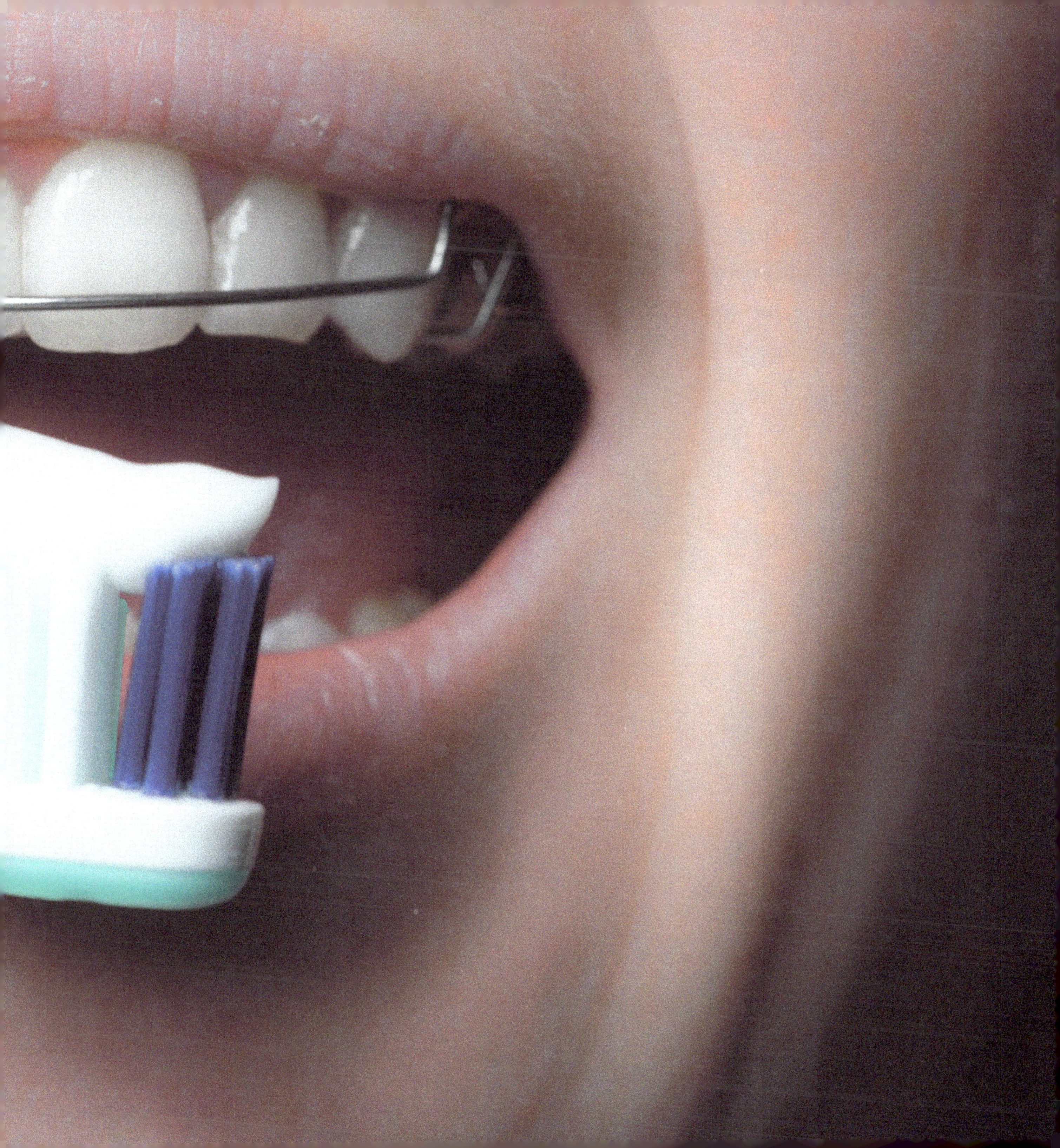

IT IS A NONMETAL

Fluorine is a light nonmetal element with the atomic number nine and symbol F. It is the lightest halogen and exists as a pale yellow diatomic gas.

It is the most electronegative element in the periodic table and highly reactive, reacting with all other elements except argon, neon, and helium. It is one of the lightest elements, but it is one of the most reactive.

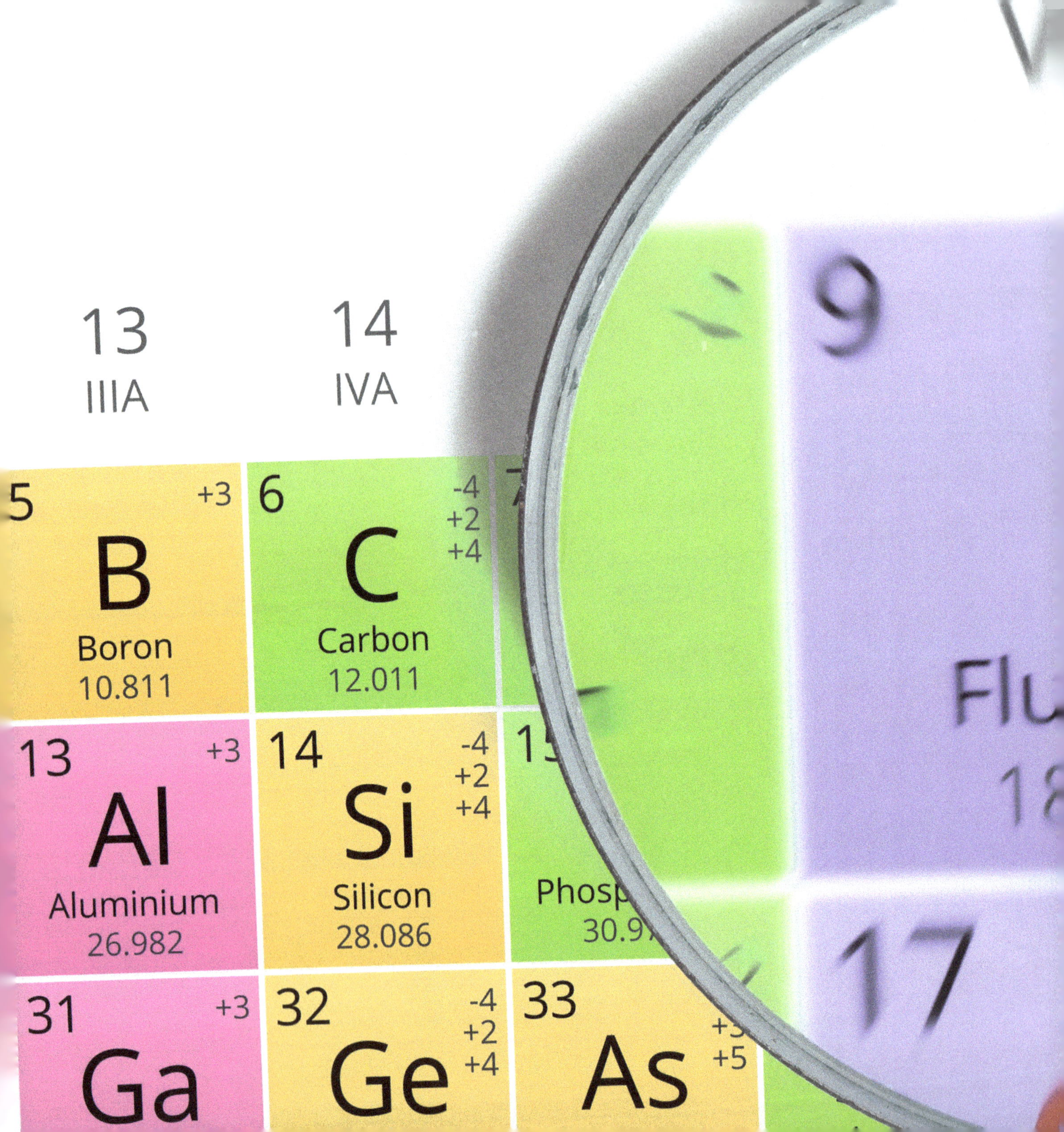
13
IIIA
14
IVA
5 +3
B
Boron
10.811
6 -4 +2 +4
C
Carbon
12.011
13 +3
Al
Aluminium
26.982
14 -4 +2 +4
Si
Silicon
28.086
31 +3
Ga
32 -4 +2 +4
Ge
33 +5
As
9
17

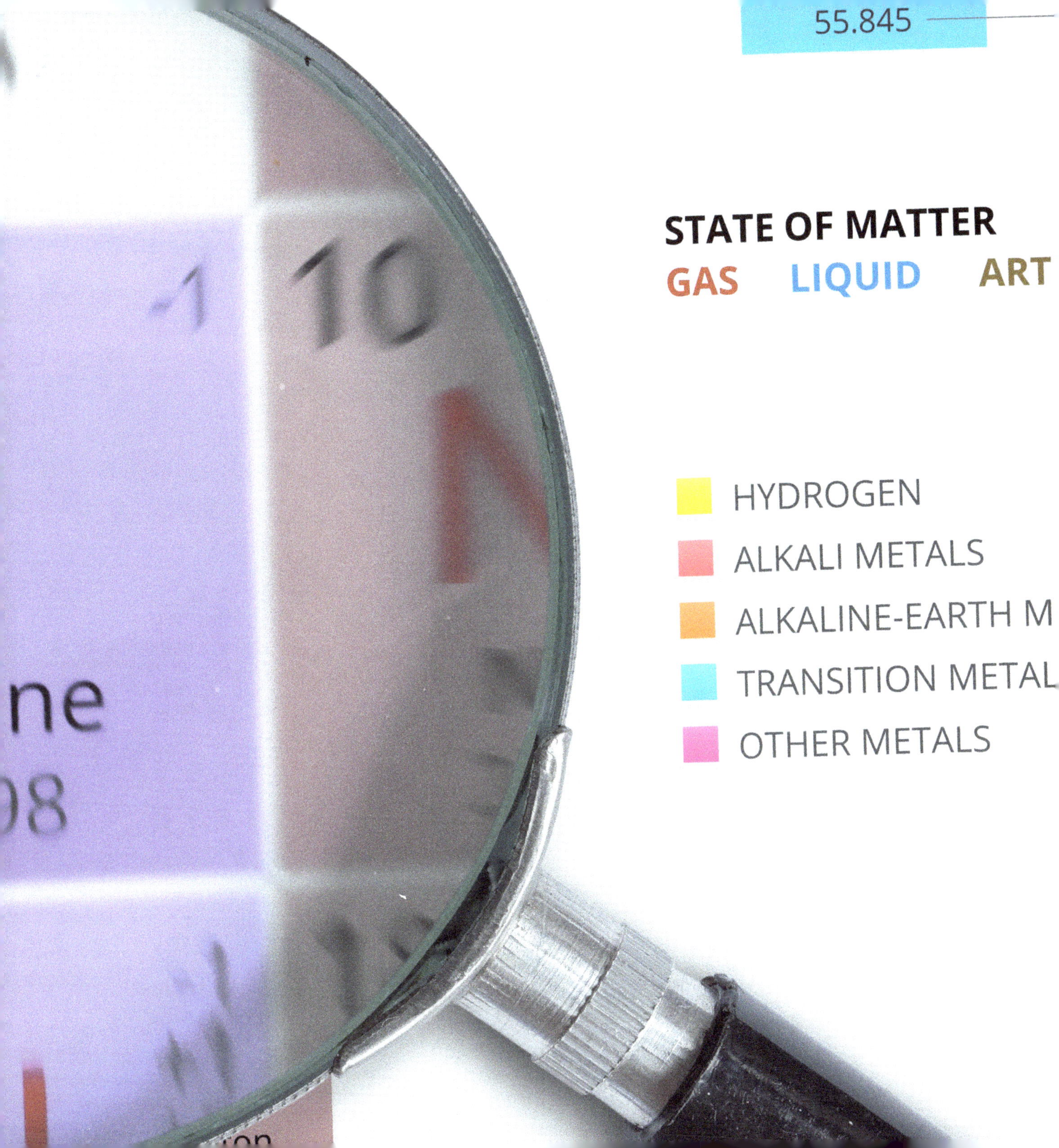
55.845
STATE OF MATTER
GAS
LIQUID
ART
HYDROGEN
ALKALI METALS
ALKALINE-EARTH M
TRANSITION METAL
OTHER METALS

Fluorine is the most reactive nonmetal element due to its electro negative properties. It can also form covalent bonds with other atoms and can react violently with oxygen.

Because of its high electronegativity, fluorine can form compounds with noble gases.

IT IS POISONOUS

Fluorine is an element that is found naturally in water and soil. It is also found in shellfish and tea.

It is a very reactive element. Fluorine is very harmful to humans because it can cause serious irritation to the respiratory system and even death. Fluoride can cause spots on teeth, especially in children.

9
F
fluorine
18.998

Fluoride accumulates in plant foliage and inhibits photosynthesis and other processes. It moves in the transpiration stream from the roots to the leaves through the stomata.

As a result, plants that have high fluoride levels suffer injury. Symptoms of fluorine damage include leaf tip necrosis and marginal necrosis.

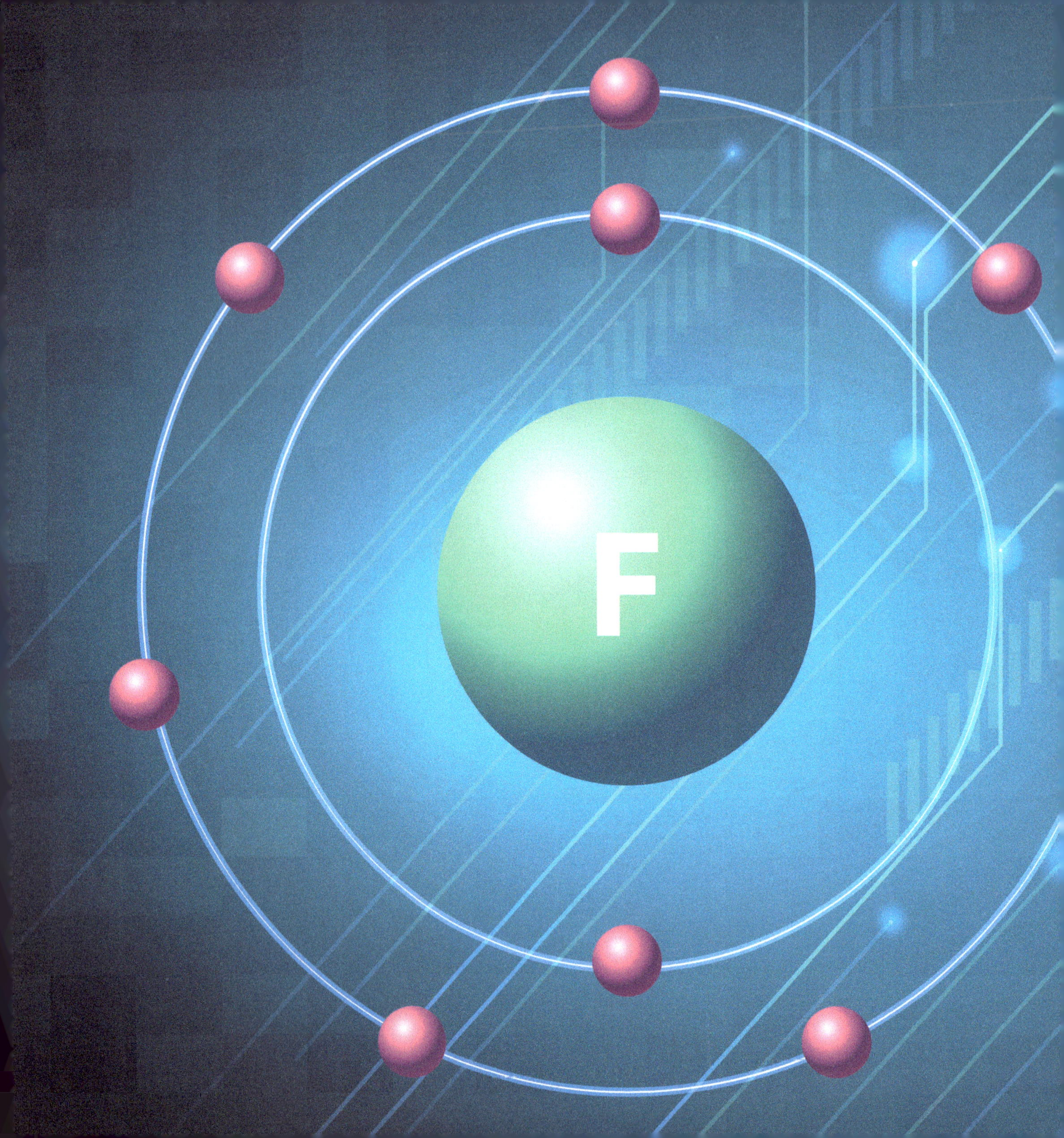
F

9
F
Fluorine
18.9984032

IT IS ELECTRONEGATIVE

Fluorine is an element with the symbol F and atomic number 9. It is the lightest halogen and is the most electronegative element.

It exists as a pale yellow diatomic gas. It is also very reactive, reacting with every other element except for argon, neon, and helium.

Fluorine has a lone electron in the outermost cell and needs just one more to go to the noble state. After accepting an electron, fluorine will have nine protons and ten electrons and will become an ion.

Fluorine is an electronegative element and its electronegativity decreases with atomic size as we move from the left to the right side of the periodic table. This makes fluorine the most reactive non-metal.

IT IS FOUND IN MINERALS

Fluorine is found in minerals and is essential for the nutrition of certain vertebrates. It forms compounds with two other elements – Na+ and K+.

This table shows how much Fluorine is present in various minerals. It also indicates the percentage of each mineral that contains Fluorine.

Fluorine is found in minerals in trace amounts. In the body, it helps maintain the crystalline structure of bones and teeth, making them less likely to break or decay.

Fluorine is important enough to make most water supplies fluoridated and is used in toothpaste and other products that use fluoride. Fluorine is mined in fluorite and other fluoride minerals, including cryolite and apatite.

IT IS USED IN ROCKET FUEL

Fluorine is an element that is found in the second period of the periodic table and is the first member of the halogen family.

It is a yellowish gas at room temperature and is highly reactive. Unlike chlorine, fluorine is toxic to humans. But, as a rocket fuel component, it is very good at facilitating explosive reactions.

In 1960s, the use of liquid fluorine in rocket fuel seemed to signal the beginning of a new generation of high-performance engines.